BOBCATS

by Arnold Ringstad

Amicus High Interest is published by Amicus
P.O. Box 1329, Mankato, MN 56002
www.amicuspublishing.us

Library of Congress Cataloging-in-Publication Data
Ringstad, Arnold, author.
 Bobcats / by Arnold Ringstad.
    pages cm. -- (Wild cats)
 Summary: "Presents information about bobcats, their habitats, and their special features, including their short bobbed tails"-- Provided by publisher.
 Audience: 6.
 Audience: K to grade 3.
 Includes bibliographical references and index.
 ISBN 978-1-60753-598-0 (hardcover) -- ISBN 978-1-60753-638-3 (pdf ebook)
 1. Bobcat--Juvenile literature. I. Title.
 QL737.C23R565 2014
 599.75'36--dc23
                               2013044188

Photo Credits: worldswildlifewonders/Shutterstock Images, cover; Tim Fitzharris/Minden Pictures/Corbis, 2, 14–15, 18–19; W. Perry Conway/Corbis, 4–5; RIRF Stock/Shutterstock Images, 6–7, 23; Mdoubrava/iStockphoto/Thinkstock, 8–9, 22; Tony Rix/Shutterstock Images, 10–11; Michael Quinton/Minden Pictures/Corbis, 12–13; cultura/Corbis, 16–17; Cordier Sylvain/Hemis/Corbis, 20–21

Produced for Amicus by The Peterson Publishing Company and Red Line Editorial.

Designer Becky Daum
Printed in the United States of America
Mankato, MN
January, 2015
PA10006
10 9 8 7 6 5 4 3 2

TABLE OF CONTENTS

Fur and Tails

Bobcats are wild cats. They have shorter tails than other cats. Short tails may help them hide from **prey**. Bobcats have spots on their fur. The spots help them blend in with the forest.

Like a Housecat?

Bobcats are about twice as big as housecats.

Bobcat Habitats

Bobcats live in North American forests. The cats like to rest on rocky ledges. They also sleep in hollow logs.

Sharp and Quiet

Bobcats have sharp claws. They can pull their claws into their paws. Then their claws do not crunch leaves on the ground. This helps them move quietly.

9

Up at Night

Bobcats are **nocturnal** animals. They sleep during the day. They are active at night. Bobcats are known for being quiet. They sneak around to surprise prey.

Hunting

Bobcats hunt rabbits and other small animals. They sneak through snow or grass. Then they pounce on their prey. Bobcats can jump 10 feet (3 m). They also can climb trees to find prey.

Living Alone

Grown-up bobcats live alone. Mothers raise kittens by themselves. Bobcats have their own **territories**. They hunt in these areas.

Baby Bobcats

Bobcat kittens weigh less than one pound (0.5 kg). Their mother keeps them safe and warm. She feeds them milk from her body.

Growing Up

Bobcat kittens drink only milk. Later, their mother brings them meat. She teaches them how to hunt. The kittens sneak through the grass. They practice **pouncing**.

Like a Housecat?

Housecats pounce on toy mice. This is like the way bobcats pounce on prey.

Protecting Bobcats

Hunters once killed many bobcats. New laws in the 1970s protected these wild cats. Bobcats now live across North America.

21

Bobcat Facts

Size: 9–30 pounds (4–14 kg), 26–41 inches (65–105 cm)

Range: North America

Habitat: forests

Number of babies: 1–6

Food: rabbits

Special feature: short tail

Words to Know

nocturnal – active at night

pouncing – jumping on

prey – animals hunted by other animals

territories – the areas animals live in and defend

Learn More

Books

Randall, Henry. *Bobcats (Cats of the Wild)*. New York: PowerKids Press, 2011.

Shea, Therese M. *Bobcats in the Dark (Creatures of the Night)*. New York: Gareth Stevens, 2012.

Websites

National Geographic—Bobcats

http://animals.nationalgeographic.com/animals/mammals /bobcat

See photos of bobcats and hear the sounds they make.

San Diego Zoo—Lynx and Bobcat

http://animals.sandiegozoo.org/animals/lynx-and-bobcat

Learn more fun facts about bobcats.

Index